To the Hot Shots
R.L.-O.

Written by Rebecca Lewis-Oakes
Illustrations by Chris Dickason
Cover typography based on designs by Thy Bui

First published in Great Britain in 2023 by Red Shed, part of Farshore

An imprint of HarperCollins*Publishers*
1 London Bridge Street, London SE1 9GF
www.farshore.co.uk

HarperCollins*Publishers*
Macken House, 39/40 Mayor Street Upper,
Dublin 1, D01 C9W8, Ireland

Copyright © HarperCollins*Publishers* Limited 2023
Illustration on page 59 is by Emiliano Migliardo

ISBN 978 0 00 864183 2
Printed and bound in the UK using 100% Renewable Electricity at CPI Group (UK) Ltd.
001

A CIP catalogue record for this title is available from the British Library.

MIX
Paper | Supporting
responsible forestry
FSC™ C007454

This book is produced from independently certified FSC™ paper
to ensure responsible forest management.

For more information visit: www.harpercollins.co.uk/green

AMAZING FACTS

THE LIONESSES

RED SHED

Did you know?

Captain Leah Williamson was the first English woman to lift a major international trophy!

The Lionesses once scored 20 goals in a single match.

Women's football was banned for 50 years!

England's youngest international player was aged just 13.

Read on to discover over 100 fascinating and surprising facts about England's UEFA EURO Championship-winning squad and the football pioneers who paved their way!

The Lionesses is the nickname given to the England women's football team.

A symbol featuring three lions represents the English nation and appears on the shirts of both the women's and men's team players. It's a fitting nickname – there is huge *pride* in the Lionesses after their historic 2022 EUROs win!

England aren't the only football team to be named after animals.

Brazil's women's team are the *Canarinhas* (female canaries), Botswana are the Zebras and Nigeria are the Super Falcons. There are more big cats too: the Dutch team are the Orange Lionesses and Cameroon are the Indomitable Lionesses!

Lionesses can run up to 80kmph!

Um, that's real lions though. The fastest female players can go over 30kmph. Lauren Hemp is one of the fastest on the England squad. The average player runs about 10km during every match!

The Lionesses were watched by almost 90,000 fans at Wembley.

On 31st July 2022, 87,192 football fans cheered the Lionesses on in the EURO 2022 final at Wembley. In front of a packed stadium, they beat Germany 2–1 to win the tournament!

The Lionesses stormed their manager's press conference... with a song!

The team interrupted Sarina Wiegman's press conference after the EUROs final, singing the song 'Sweet Caroline' and even jumping on the table!

The Lionesses scored a total of 22 goals at the EUROs.

And they sang 'Sweet Caroline' to celebrate many of them!

Beth Mead was the top scorer at the EURO 2022 Championships.

She wowed fans with six goals and five assists. Go, Beth!

Fellow Lioness Alessia Russo was the tournament's third top goal-scorer with four goals and one assist.

Alessia Russo also won Goal of the Tournament.

This award is voted for by fans. Alessia won for her awesome back-heel, back-of-the-net goal against Sweden. The Lionesses scored five out of the top ten Goals of the Tournament at the 2022 EUROs!

Sarina Wiegman is a super coach.

With Wiegman as their manager, the Lionesses didn't lose a match for two whole years, from April 2021 until April 2023!

Sarina is the first coach to win back-to-back EUROs with different teams.

Wiegman led her native Netherlands to victory in 2017, and moved to run the England squad in 2021, winning the very next EUROs in 2022. Go, Sarina!

Sarina was also a star player.

Before turning to coaching, Sarina won 104 caps for the Netherlands as a midfielder. She was the first female player to reach a century (that's 100) appearances for her country.

Sarina was named Best FIFA Women's Coach in 2022.

It was the THIRD time she had won this award. No one else has even won it twice. She really is a super coach!

Leah Williamson was the first English woman to lift a major international football trophy.

Literally! As captain, she got her hands on the UEFA Women's EURO trophy first.

Leah has played international football at every age.

Leah Williamson played at every single England age group from Under 15s up to professional.

Leah was eating a meal at Nandos when she got the call-up for England's EURO 2022 squad.

Her favourite pre-match meal is a ham sandwich!

Modern English football began in the 1800s.

But ever since the ball was invented, people have been kicking it around! There's evidence of ball sports being played in Ancient China and Ancient Greece.

Balls have even been found in Egyptian tombs from way back in 2,500BCE!

One of the earliest public women's football matches was North versus South.

It was played at Hornsey, north London, in 1885 and drew a crowd of 10,000 people. The team calling itself 'North' beat 'South' 7–1.

Female footballers used to wear 'knickerbockers'!

Pioneering female footballers blazed a fashion trail in loose blouses, 'knickerbockers' (a bit like baggy shorts), stockings, boots and caps.

For a long time, women had to play football unofficially.

The original English FA (Football Association) was formed in 1863 and it established the FA Cup in 1872. Originally there were 50 official member clubs – all for men! But women's teams still played unofficially, in front of huge crowds.

Emma Clarke was a pioneering Black female footballer.

When she played for South in the famous match in Hornsey, Emma became the first recorded Black female football player. Emma and her sister, Jane, also played for a team called Mrs Graham's XI in Bootle, Liverpool. It was named after local renowned suffragist, and footballer, Helen Graham Matthews.

Women's football flourished during World War I.

The FA suspended the men's league in 1915 because so many young men had been called up to fight in World War I (1914–1918). Women were doing many jobs previously done by men, and some set up football teams at work. Dick Kerr's munitions factory in Preston, Lancashire, had one of the best known teams: Dick Kerr Ladies.

Dick Kerr Ladies became famous after winning a match against a men's side!

The team was so good, they drew a crowd of thousands.

On Boxing Day, 1920, they beat St Helen's 4–0. More than 53,000 spectators crowded into Goodison Park stadium and 10,000 more were turned away!

Dick Kerr Ladies played the first women's international game in England, beating a French side 2–0.

Dick Kerr Ladies were the first team to play at night.

The War Office wanted to encourage women's football, so they supplied the team with a white ball and floodlights so they could play on in the dark!

Women's football was banned for 50 years!

After WWI, men who had been on the battlefield returned to their old jobs – and the football pitch. On 5th December 1921, the English FA banned women from training or competing in their grounds because the women's game was proving to be TOO popular – the FA wanted the crowds to return to the men's game.

**The ban was officially overturned
in 1971. Phew!**

Football has always been TOO MUCH FUN!

It's not just the women's game that has been banned in the past. In 1314, the Lord Mayor of London banned ALL football for causing 'chaos' in the capital!

The beautiful game annoyed a king.

In fact, it annoyed several! Kings Edward II, Richard II, Henry IV and Henry V all made football illegal, claiming it distracted their soldiers during the Hundred Years War (1337–1453).

Footie matches haven't always been 90 minutes long – or played on a pitch!

In medieval times, some games used to run ALL DAY. In England, it was called 'mob football' and could be played over an entire town. The winning team was the one with the ball at the end of the day. It's thought that women had their own mob football games, separate from the men.

Today the men's and women's games are . . . exactly the same!

Unlike in some other sports, there is just one set of international rules for football, for both the men's and women's games.

Footballs are always the same size.

Yes, all adult football teams play with a ball that is the exact same size. It's called a size 5, and its circumference must measure between 68cm and 70cm.

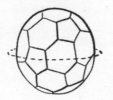

Some footballs have bells inside.

Blind football, or futsal, is played with a ball that contains a noise-maker like a bell so that players can hear it coming.

The Lionesses once scored 20 goals in a single match.

It's true! The game was a 2023 FIFA Women's World Cup qualifier against Latvia. This epic score broke the previous records set by the men's AND women's senior England teams.

Four players each scored a hat-trick!

Three goals scored by the same player in a single match is called a 'hat-trick'. Ellen White, Beth Mead, Alessia Russo and Lauren Hemp ALL scored three goals in the match against record-breaking match against Latvia!

Lauren Hemp scored a 'super hat-trick'.

A 'super hat-trick' is FOUR goals from one player in one match. Lauren already had a hat-trick, then snuck in one last goal to end the game. GOOAAAAAL!

Fara Williams has 172 caps for England.

Football players (and players of some others sports too) earn a 'cap' for every international game they play. Former Lioness Fara Williams played for England a whopping 172 times – and scored 40 international goals!

Jill Scott is England's second most capped Lioness.

The former Lioness has 161 caps. Fara and Jill both have more caps than Peter Shilton, England's most capped men's player, who achieved 125 caps from 1970 to 1990.

Jill Scott is Queen of the Jungle . . .

Jill Scott played from 2006 to 2022, retiring just after the EUROs win. She immediately went on to win reality TV show *I'm a Celebrity . . . Get Me Out of Here!*

. . . and she's the queen of silly celebrations too.

After the 2022 EUROs win, Jill 'interviewed' the trophy in front of crowds in London's Trafalgar Square.

Ellen White is England's top scorer.

Former Lioness Ellen White hit a superhuman 52 balls on target for England. Former players Kelly Smith and Kerry Davis are close behind with 46 and 44 goals each. The current squad had better get busy with those records to beat!

Lionesses never sleep!

Even when they retire from the pitch, you'll see plenty of Lionesses still involved in the beautiful game. Alex Scott played 140 international games from 2004 to 2017, including the London 2012 Olympics. She's now a top sports commentator on the BBC and other channels.

Jordan Nobbs is from a footballing family.

The Aston Villa star's dad, Keith, played professionally for Hartlepool United. While Jordan plays in midfield, and regularly scores for England, Keith played in defence. He did manage to put the ball into the back of the net just once for Hartlepool though!

Even injury couldn't keep Jordan Nobbs away from the 2019 World Cup.

Jordan tore her ACL (heel ligament) – ouch! She couldn't play for the Lionesses but still travelled to France to appear as a TV pundit!

Jordan Nobbs and Demi Stokes have played together ever since they were seven.

They met on a trial day for Sunderland and have been teammates ever since!

Ella Toone was a footballing baby!

When baby Ella was only a few days old, her dad took her to a local match. His side, Hindsford, were a player short, so he went onto the pitch, leaving Ella in her pram. But the ball went over the touchline, knocking over the pram. Ella fell out onto the grass – and from that day on, her dad would say that his daughter was destined to be a footballer!

The greatest female footballer of all time is nicknamed 'Pelé in skirts'.

Marta Vieira da Silva, known to fans as 'Marta', was named FIFA World Player of the Year a massive SIX times: five times in a row from 2006 to 2010, and again in 2018. Pelé – in case you didn't know – was a legendary Brazilian footballer, who regarded Marta so highly, he gave her the nickname himself!

**26th October is
Rainbow Laces Day!**

Whoever you're in a relationship with, it's no big deal in women's football. Lots of high-profile England women's players have come out as LGBTQ+, including Lily Parr, Lianne Sanderson, Casey Stoney, Kelly Smith, Fara Williams and Beth Mead. Rainbow Laces Day celebrates LGBTQ+ inclusion in all sports.

The Lionesses have THREE reasons to celebrate on 2nd February.

Three current and former Lionesses share a birthday on this date: Jill Scott, Faye White and Gabby George. Happy birthday, Lionesses!

Jill Scott nearly did a runner.

She was the North of England under 13 cross-country champion and won the Junior Great North Run, before deciding to focus on football. She also studied sport at Loughborough University. Who knows what sport Jill might move on to next?!

A bus driver put women's football on the map.

Bus driver Harry Batt and his wife, June, founded the Chiltern Valley Ladies' team in Luton in 1969, and quickly took them international. FIEFF (the Federation of Indepedent European Female Football) invited the team to play in Italy that year, making them the first English women's team ever to play overseas. Game-changer!

The youngest ever Lioness was just 13.

Midfielder Leah Caleb was selected for the England team that travelled to Mexico for the first unofficial World Cup in 1971.

China hosted the first OFFICIAL Women's World Cup!

It wasn't until 1991 that FIFA (the international governing body for association football) established the first official World Cup tournament for women. Finally!

The Lionesses have qualified for the FIFA Women's World Cup six times.

The squad competed in 1995, 2007, 2011, 2015, 2019 and 2023.

They reached the quarter-finals three times.

The Lionesses played Germany in the semis in 1995, USA in 2007 and France in 2011.

They reached the semi-finals twice.

The Lionesses were beaten by Japan in 2015 and the USA in 2019. Both tournaments were won by the USA.

Keira Walsh became the most expensive female player of all time.

The Lioness midfielder was bought from Manchester City by Barcelona for a record fee of around £400,000 in 2022. Kerching!

Lauren James broke records at just 19.

When Chelsea bought the teenage striker for £200,000 in 2021, it was a record transfer fee between two Women's Super League clubs. Better still? Lauren's brother, Reece, also plays for Chelsea!

Georgia Stanway is the foulest England player.

Well, she recorded the most fouls on the team in the 2022 EUROs: ten. It was the third highest tally in the whole competition. And she got two yellow cards – oops!

Lucy Bronze has ALL the trophies...

She was the first English player to win UEFA Women's Player of the Year in 2018/19. She also won Best FIFA Women's Player of the Year in 2020. At her clubs, she has won every UK championship title, playing at Sunderland, Liverpool, Everton and Manchester City. And if that wasn't enough, she moved to France in 2017 and helped Lyon win the Champions League AND the French league. Her trophy shelf must be groaning by now!

. . . but at university, she spent more time serving pizza than on the pitch!

It's true! She worked in an Italian restaurant while studying AND playing for Everton.

Beth Mead is so clever, she has a university scholarship named after her.

Mead studied for her degree in Sports Development at Teesside University while playing for Sunderland. Together with the university, she launched a scholarship to support students who are also pursuing professional women's football. What a way to secure the next EURO Championships!

Beth Mead ALSO has an octopus named after her!

Staff at the Sea Life Centre in Scarborough named the football-loving octopus after the Lionesses star in celebration of the team's 2022 EUROs win!

Beth Mead is a champion egg thrower.

True story! In 2015, Beth won the first Yorkshire
Open Egg Throwing Championships.

Beth and her friend Rachel Laws, also
a footballer, competed with several other
teams to see who could throw their egg the
furthest – and catch it! Their winning throw
was an EGGCEPTIONAL 50m!

Bethany England has a talented twin.

Her twin sister, Laura, is an international athlete who has competed for Team GB at the Olympics.

As children, Beth and Laura played football in a team called Junior Tykes. They lost their first match by more than 20 goals!

Leah Williamson is the team DJ.

When the Lionesses are preparing for a big match, it's Leah who chooses the tunes that will motivate them. Yes, she *does* take requests!

The tallest Lioness is 1.78m.

Esme Morgan and Lotte Wubben-Moy are among the tallest players on the England squad. At 1.88m (6'2"), Wendie Rennard of France is the tallest female player in the world.

There's only one . . . left-footer.

In the 2022 EURO squad, every single player listed their preferred foot as right – except for defender Alex Greenwood, who's a leftie! Did you know left-handers are sometimes considered more creative? Well, it seems left-footers are too!

Niamh Charles is ambidextrous.

Amazing word? Amazing woman!
Defender Niamh doesn't prefer her right foot –
she's equally great on both feet! Now there's
a champion.

Fara Williams has coached for the Homeless FA charity.

Having experienced homelessness herself during her early football career, Fara is committed to giving back. She even helped select the England team for the charity tournament 'Homeless World Cup'. She was awarded an MBE in 2016 for services to football and charity. What a star.

Bob Marley's daughter funds the Jamaican women's football team.

Women's sports are underfunded across the world. In Jamaica, the daughter of reggae musician Bob Marley took matters into her own hands to raise money for the national team. Cedella Marley released a song in their honour and campaigned for better funding. She's Number One!

Lucy Bronze's middle name is tough.

Yes, really! Her full name is
Lucy Roberta Tough Bronze!

Lauren Hemp's nickname is Hempo.

Maybe not the most original name, but Lauren's skills on the pitch are another level. She won the FA's Young Player of the Year award in 2018, 2019, 2020 AND 2022.

Nikita Parris's nickname is Keets.

The Lioness and Manchester United star comes from a sporting family. Her sister, Natasha Jonas, is a professional boxer!

Goalie Mary Earps is known as Mazza or Mearps.

Growing up, Mearps says she was the only player on her girls teams who liked shouting, or even talking, on the pitch!

Ella Toone still goes to school.

Well, sort of! She loved her time at Fred Longworth High School so much, and appreciates how supportive her PE teachers were, that when she's home, she'll go in and play five-a-side with the teachers!

Demi Stokes used to buy her own trophies.

When they played football on the estate she grew up on, Demi and her friends organised their own mini tournaments. They would all contribute a few pounds to buy a trophy for the winners!

Alessia Russo has a sock-er superstition.

Alessia will always put her right sock, boot and shinpad on before her left. Then, when she's on the pitch, just before the whistle blows to start the match, she jumps SEVEN times, really high, for good luck!

Keira Walsh always puts her shinpads on the opposite legs before a big match.

She first did it by accident; now it's a superstition she can't change!

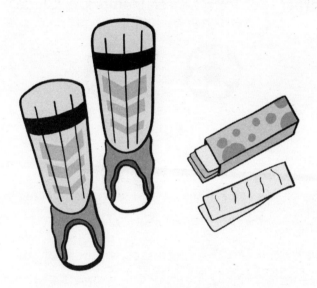

Niamh Charles HAS to chew gum.

Before a match, Niamh has a ritual gum chew, then she gets rid of it halfway through the warm-up.

Chloe Kelly won at Wembley . . .

Chloe scored the winning goal at the 2022
EUROs, played at Wembley stadium, off
a corner shot from Lauren Hemp. Go, Chloe!

. . . twice!

She also scored the winning penalty in
the first ever Finalissima, which took place
at Wembley in April 2023.

The match saw the Lionesses, winners of the
Women's EURO, beat Brazil, winners of the
Copa América Femenina. The score was 1–1
at full-time with England eventually winning
4–2 on penalties.

Chloe almost missed the EUROs final.

She was recovering from a serious knee injury before the EUROs. Chloe credited the England physio team with getting her back on her feet and on the pitch just in time to score that incredible winning goal in extra time!

Sheila Parker was the first official England Women's captain.

She captained the 1972 WFA (Women's Football Association) team, leading our Lionesses to victory in the first ever home nations championship in 1976. That's a lot of firsts!

Lily Parr was the first female player to be inducted into the National Football Museum Hall of Fame.

She scored almost 1,000 goals during her career. Even more astonishing – she played for thirty years! That's far longer than players today . . .

Hope Powell was headline news.

The former Lioness scored a sensational 35 goals in 66 matches. But she became famous long before scoring for England . . .

In the 1970s, the FA banned girls over the age of 11 from playing for boys' teams. Hope's teacher appealed the ban, and the story was widely reported. But it wasn't about feminism – Hope was the best player and he wanted the team to win!

Hope has more football firsts than almost any other Lioness.

In 1995, Hope won a spot on the England team aged just 16. (She wasn't paid though – female players even had to buy their own boots!)

She was named manager of the England women's team in 1998. She was the first woman AND the first person of colour to hold the role. She was also the youngest ever England manager.

Hope joined the National Football Hall of Fame in 2003 – only the second woman after footballing pioneer Lily Parr. Amazing!

The first Women's World Cup games were only 80 minutes long.

For no particular reason. Shortly after, the games were extended to 90 minutes, which is now standard in all football matches.

England men and women are nearly equal in FIFA rankings.

The men are ranked 5th but the women are 4th!

Former Lioness Gill Coultard was the first female player to reach 100 caps.

She also captained the Lionesses from 1991. Go, Gill!

12th July 2022 saw an extraordinary score in a EUROs group match.

The Lionesses beat their previous goal difference record (6–0 against Scotland in 2017) by two goals to win a clear 8–0 over Norway in the EUROs group stage. No side has ever scored eight goals in a EURO Championship match before – men's or women's!

The Lionesses are now virtual.

In 2023, the esports FIFA game is finally including the best women's players in the world for the first time! Look out for the virtual Lionesses Lucy Bronze, Beth Mead, Lauren Hemp, Leah Williamson, and many more!

Mary Earps isn't just light on her feet, she's a twinkletoes too.

Mary played lots of sports as a child, from badminton and judo to swimming and dancing. She even had a solo to 'Pop Goes the Weasel' in a show when she was 11!

Mary played so much football as a child, she wore out her shoes.

Her mum was cross at how many pairs of shoes Mary went through in a school year! But we're glad for all the awesome practice it gave her.

Mary almost quit football before the EUROs.

She played against Germany in November 2019 at Wembley but was not called up to the side again for another two years. In 2021, Mary considered retiring, but coach Sarina Wiegman arrived and brought her back on the pitch. Hurrah!

Fran Kirby wasn't allowed to play football at school.

She was too good! Fran played for Reading Academy from the age of seven. Her best friend also played for a club team. When they were on the school team together, no one else could beat them – so they were banned from competing. Noooo!

Fran started out in goal.

As a kid, Fran loved playing in goal. But she also loved coming out to score goals. At about 12, she became a winger before moving to midfield.

Her girls-only team played in a boys league.

Fran's team, Caversham United, finished second in their league!

Today, Fran is in a league of her own!

She has five Women's Super League championship wins to her name, as well as her many Lioness victories.

Alessia Russo scored the fastest hat-trick in Lioness history.

During England's astonishing 20–0 win over Latvia in the 2023 World Cup qualifier, Alessia came on as a sub. She quickly – VERY quickly – scored a hat-trick. Taking just 11 minutes, it's the fastest three goals by a Lioness ever!

Alessia Russo and Lotte Wubben-Roy studied together at the University of North Carolina.

They both played for the legendary North Carolina Tar Heels team. But despite playing in America, they still call it 'football' not 'soccer'!

Alessia almost failed her Geology class because of her England call-up.

True story! Then-manager Phil Neville called to tell her the good news that she had been selected for the England squad, but because of the time difference between the UK and USA, Alessia was sitting in a Geology lecture. She left the class and was too excited to return!

Georgia Stanway played alongside her hero.

Midfielder Georgia Stanway was inspired by World Cup champion and Olympic gold medallist Carli Lloyd. The two women were Manchester City teammates in 2017. Carli gave Georgia a pair of signed boots when she left the club, telling her to go and 'do something special'.

Nikita Parris's biggest heroes were Julie Fleeting and Thierry Henry.

Watching Scottish football legend Julie Fleeting in the FA cup inspired young Nikita to want to become the best female footballer in the world. Who are YOUR football heroes?

Could you be one of the next generation of Lionesses?

Only 63% of UK schools currently provide equal access to football for girls through PE lessons. So nearly a THIRD of our potential future Lionesses don't have the chance to play. Schools must change this, now!

FIFA wants to double the number of female players worldwide.

By 2026, FIFA wants 60 million women and girls joining the beautiful game. LET'S GO!

Look out for other books in the series!

KING CHARLES III

SIR DAVID ATTENBOROUGH

THE LIONESSES